We Will Always Be My Favorite Love Story

Ravenwolf

Copyright © 2022 by The Ravenwolf Group

All rights reserved. This book or any portion thereof may not be reproduced or used in any manner whatsoever without the express written permission of the publisher except for the use of brief quotations in a book review or the like.

First Paperback Edition: January 2022

ISBN: 979-8-88525-457-1 (print)
ISBN: 979-8-88525-458-8 (e-book)

Hyperbole Publishing
www.houseofravenwolf.com

Love Stories

We're Not Perfect, but
We're Perfect for Each Other 11

Promise Me That This Is Forever 12

All I Need Is You Needing Me 14

Hugs From Behind 16

Take Me with You....................................... 18

There Are No Accidental
Meetings Between Souls............................ 20

When I Really Need It 22

I Choose … 24

Happy Together.. 26

In Search of Life 28

Safe.. 30

I Want to Set My Soul on Fire..................... 34

When Our Lips Meet and Souls Connect,
Nothing Else Matters 38

Long Before I Ever Met You 40

I Never Knew Love
Until I Was Loved by You 43

Loving You Endlessly 45

When Our Faces Are Lined with Wrinkles
from a Life Well Lived 47

Love Is the Person You Miss When
Surrounded by Friends 48

You're the Person
I Want to Come Home To 50

In a World Full of Wrongs, You Choose
to Always See What Is Right 52

The Best Love Makes You Better 55

When All That Really Matters
Is That You're Together 57

Moments Like These 59

One Moment Can Change Your Life,
One Love Can Change Your World 61

Soulfully in Sync 63

Our Souls Are the Same 66

You Will Forever Be My Always 68

The Heart Knows
When the Search Is Over 70

Afraid of the Realness 73

And I Choose You 76

She Was a Warm Embrace, His Reminder
of Beauty in the World 78

I Would Wait for You Forever 80

Show Me Your Truth and
Then Let Me Love You 83

Kiss Her as if You are
Writing Poetry on Her Soul 86

Here and Where You Are 87

I Choose Both 89

Every Time I Follow My Heart
It Leads Me to You 91

Your Love Feels Like Sunshine 93

Wild and Free 95

One Person Can Show You That
All People Are Not the Same 98

Already Fallen 102

When I Still Tasted Like Heartbreak 104

There Are Not Enough Stars 107

Finding the Small Miracles
Among the Ordinary 110

The Enchanting Cocoon
of Your Loving Embrace 113

I Didn't Know What to Wish for …
Until You 115

Once in a While,
Love Gives Us a Fairy Tale 117

Stand Under the Stars with Me Forever .. 121

Look for Someone Who Won't Let You
Face the World Alone 124

We Fall in Love by Chance,
We Stay in Love by Choice 126

Life Needs More Slow Dances,
Stolen Kisses and Quiet Moments 127

You Don't Want the Stars,
so I'll Bring You the Ocean Instead 129

You Have Me 132

You Did Something for Me I Couldn't Do for
Myself. You Loved Me for Who I Am 134

I Can't Promise to Fix All of Your Problems,
but I Can Promise You Won't Have to Face
Them Alone 136

Thank You for Reminding Me What
Butterflies Feel Like 138

You Make My Heart Smile
When Nothing Else Can 140

To Truly Be in Love 142

Those Quiet Times When the World Just Melts Away 145

I Want You Forever 147

So Much More than Those
Three Little Words 149

Freeze Time 151

The Heart that Beats Only for You 153

And I Wonder, How Did I Find One
So Perfect for Me? 155

Love Like Fairy Tales Do Come True...... 158

Forgetting Yesterday &
Dreaming of Tomorrow........................... 161

I Don't Want the Moon …
I Want to Love and Be Loved 164

Love Her So Much that She May Doubt
Your Sanity … But Never Your Passion .. 166

Hold My Hand and Don't Ever Let Me Go 168

True Love is Worth the Wait.................... 170

To Laugh Forever with Someone
You Take Seriously 173

I Need You with Me 175

The One Who Completes You.................. 177

Her Anchor, His Wings 178

Every Time She Laughs 181

Love Itself Isn't Enough
to Make Forever Possible......................... 183

Now and For Always 186

We Will Always Be
My Favorite Love Story 188

We're Not Perfect, but We're Perfect for Each Other

And all I ever wanted, I found wonderfully in you.

A perfect love between two imperfect people – finding each other against impossible odds across worlds apart.

Two souls, one heartbeat in a meeting 'twixt the stars above … always meant to be and forever joined in a love without end.

Perfectly imperfect together – and I'd have it no other way.

That's the best happily ever after I could ask for …

Meant to be, real and forever.

Promise Me That This Is Forever

My love,
Promise me that this is forever.
Promise me that no matter what tomorrow brings,
It will find me in your arms.
Promise me that we will face everything together, hand in hand.
Promise me that we will always have silly times and mad laughter.
Promise me that you'll always be my refuge from a world that sometimes hurts.
Promise me that we will always remember to put each other first.
Promise me that we'll never go to bed without each other and never let a fight linger.
Promise me that you'll love me for me and always be true to yourself and me.
Promise me the love to last for all ages, until I find you in the next life.
Promise me that I can always count on you, to be all the things we need.

Promise me that you'll protect my heart, nurture my soul and nourish my spirit.

Promise me that we will always remember, every day, why we fell in love ... and do it all over again.

Promise me that when the hairs go gray and wrinkles line my face, that you'll love me as you always have.

Promise me that you'll never give up on us, no matter what challenges arise.

Promise me that you'll always respect you, me and us.

Most of all ...

Just promise me that this love is the one.

The last promise I'll ever want ...

Is to be loved by you, forever.

That's the only promise I'll ever need from you, Now and for always.

All I Need Is You Needing Me

Darling,

Make no mistake about why I love you.

It's not about the things we have, the places we go or the activities we do together.

It's so much more than that.

It's just you that I need and want, without the fancy outfits or expensive accessories.

The person that I love beneath all the glitz and grandeur.

Real love doesn't need expensive gifts or grandiose jewelry and watches,

Extravagant trips or fancy things – those are all grand ideas,

But they'll never come close to what matters.

It's simple, really.

You and me, nothing more and nothing less.

Today, tomorrow and forever.

I want to feel you pressed against me,

I yearn to immerse myself in the connection between your soul and mine ...

I crave your heart beating as one with my own.

Two becomes one in every way that matters.

Forget what the world thinks.

I'll always fight for your love and the things that you value most ...

What I truly need is you needing me.

What happens in the quiet of the night,

When we are snuggled up close,

That's the feeling I can't live without ...

The love that covers me whenever you're by my side –

The happiness and joy you bring me is more than mere words can ever describe.

All I really want is to spend the rest of my life,

Waking up next to you.

If home is where the heart is,

Then I belong with you.

Because you had my heart ...

From the first moment I saw you.

You have always been and always will be ...

my happily ever after.

Hugs From Behind

There's just something special about when I wrap my arms around you from behind,

a myriad of feelings sweeps over me that words fail to convey.

The warmth of your body pressed to mine, our hearts beating in unison … well, that's just the start.

Perhaps it's all the things that your embrace tells me without saying a word.

Your arms tell me that you're there for me, through good times and bad, no matter what comes our way.

I just feel safe in those moments when I'm engrossed in you – your touch and scent seemingly make the world melt away as I drift off into all that is you.

You immersed into me, nuzzling me with delicate kisses – as if the promises of your love are woven into each sweet touch.

The feeling of being completely lost in you is an experience unlike any other.

Your arms wrapped tightly about me, your skin pressed to mine, those are the moments that I'll always treasure.

It's those times when the serenity of the starry night has breathed its last gasp into the fading day that our love is limitless.

Two souls unified into a singular consciousness that eclipses the realm of the ordinary ... that is us in those moments.

Hugs from behind.

Something so simple that can set your soul on fire,

Make your heart race,

Yet all the while soothing your spirit

And calming your mind.

That's something I want from you ...

For the rest of our lives.

Take Me with You

I don't care where we go,
Or what we do,
So long as I'm by your side,
With love in our hearts.

We don't know what tomorrow will bring,
For it is never promised,
So, let's live in this moment,
Until our love overflows with emotion.

The world around us can fall apart
And time may cease to be,
But so long as I have your hand in mine,
There's nothing we can't do.

So, let's soak in the beauty of today,
Let's lose ourselves in a cocoon of love,
Cherishing, kissing and relishing each other,
Letting passion completely overwhelm our senses.

Let's jump off the edge of today

Into an oblivion of love's doing.
No matter how far we go
Or how long it takes,

Or how hard we love ...
We will always have each other,
Heart to heart, deeply in love ...
Forever and always we will truly be.

There Are No Accidental Meetings Between Souls

I don't believe in luck, accidents or chance.

I didn't find you by sheer possibility, you were always the one meant for me.

I didn't always know your face or name, as we were written so long ago in the stars.

From the first moment I saw your face, the very instant I heard your voice, I just knew.

It's hard to describe how you know until you do.

There aren't words for how deeply I feel for you or any way I could ever truly convey how much you mean to me.

You've changed my life and calmed my soul in a way that I didn't even know I needed.

So, when people remark about how lucky I am or the good fortune I had in finding you, I just smile and nod.

When you finally find the one meant for you, you realize that chance doesn't exist, because we belong together, and always will.

The way our souls connect, the manner in which our hearts collide and the passion we feel isn't anything other than meant to be ...

And I plan on spending the rest of my life showing you just how beautiful you are to me.

When I Really Need It

I know I'm not the easiest person to love sometimes; I can be an emotional basket case some days ...

But I don't ever mean to be.

I've always loved you so very deeply, and I appreciate how you've stood by me through it all.

I realize that there are going to be those days when I push your patience to the limit with my constant upheaval of emotions, frustrations and wild moods.

Always remember that behind my dizzying array of tears, loud words and sometimes crazy ideas is a person who loves you dearly.

We've come so far together – our life and love has grown so much that I don't have the words to express my thankfulness for you ...

How you treat me with delicate care sometimes and how you seem to know just what I need when I need it ... it brings tears to my eyes.

I'm a challenge, a beautiful mess and some kind of wonderful chaos, but I'm all yours, and beneath all of my wacky ways and random moods is a person who can't imagine life without you.

Those times when life gets me down and I'm coming up for air?

That's when I'm so grateful you're there, holding out your hand.

I know that come what may, we will stand beside each other, heart to heart and soul to soul ...

It won't always be easy, and it won't always be painless ...

But our love will be worth it ...

Always and forever ...

Thank you for always having my back when I need it most.

I don't know how everyone else's love stories go, but because of you, ours will always be my favorite.

I Choose …

I'm taking this chance to love you now, soaking up this moment and immersing myself in your affection.

Tomorrow isn't promised to any of us, so I'm going to seize this day …

To accept you unconditionally,

love you unendingly and

cherish you adoringly.

I'm giving you my whole heart and soul, for without great risk, there cannot be great love.

Let's do all the things we've always dreamt of … appreciating all the small moments of our love that make our hearts smile.

Losing ourselves in the powerful sensations of our love …

Kissing in the warm afternoon rain,

Cuddling in the crisp morning air,

Holding hands as we watch the sunset fade into oblivion.

I want to know all of you in the ways I know myself …

Naked and bare, my soul is connected to yours in the most intimate ways I never knew possible.

Your heart in my hands, I will always protect and honor you with fierce devotion and protective loyalty.

Most of all, I want to experience you in all the ways the world will never know ...

The soul filling, passionate loving and deepest truths knowing that meld our heart beats into one.

We were always meant to be, and such shall we always remain.

Two souls that found each other against impossible odds and from miles apart ...

Our spirits connected and our hearts intertwined as love blessed us, at long last.

Tomorrow may never come, and the stars may fall from the night sky, but I'll use my last breaths to utter the words of just how very much I love you ...

And I always will.

Our forever will always be my favorite love story.

Happy Together

As I look over at your still form, I can't help but smile as I watch you sleep.

In that moment, all I know is that my heart is full.

My whole world is beside me, peacefully lost in slumber, and there's nothing more I could wish for.

We've been inseparable since we met, even if one of us is lost in sleep.

Those are the times when everything just feels right:

The world is quiet, and the night is serene as I softly stroke your hair with the rise and fall of your breaths.

I could stay in this feeling forever as my soul sighs, content and at peace as I feel you against me.

You're all I could have ever asked for and much more ... you've changed my world just by being a part of it.

All the things I feel and want to say flash through my mind as I watch you sleep ...

I'm just so thankful for you – the life and love we share is special in ways words can't describe.

They say it's the big things that are important, but as I look over at you, I'd tell you the little things are just as noteworthy ...

As I soak in the beauty of this moment, I know that these are the memories and feelings that will fill my heart ...

For the rest of my days ...

And in those days, I will love you always.

In Search of Life

For so very long, I sought love,
Around every corner and in everyone I met.
I didn't how and when I'd find the one
Meant for me to love and hold for always.

Time passed and my heart was torn apart,
Many times over and deeper each time,
I traveled the broken roads, looking for the love
That I found so wonderfully in you.

I wasn't waiting for love any longer,
As time had moved on and my hopes were dimmed,
I had despaired and started thinking, sadly,
That maybe, love wasn't meant for me.

Instead, I began to better myself and find the love
For whom and what I could become,
Each and every day chasing and falling in love
With myself and being alive in every moment.

So, on that fateful day when our eyes met,
And I knew the answer to all the questions
I had always asked in search of love ...
I realized in an instant you were the one.

The universe has a way of working things out
When you least expect it in ways unforeseen.
And I as look at you now, heart in my hands,
I'm reminded ...

Why I'm so thankful it never worked out with anyone else ...
Because we were always meant to be.

Safe

Laying in your arms, I tried to find the words ... any words to describe this – you – us.

I couldn't.

Your body pressed against mine, bodies seamless as our hearts pulsed to the same rhythm ... in that instant, the world was perfect.

The beauty of the moment, the timeless perfection of your angelic form embraced in my grasp ... to describe the feelings in that moment?

Beautifully impossible.

There were no words, in this language or another, that could begin to describe the powerful emotions that enveloped our souls, seemingly suspended in time.

I thought back to the sleepless nights spent alone, often desolate and bereft of hope ... a solitary tear escaped down my cheek as I wondered why ...

Why I saw couples everywhere, yet,

was I not deserving of someone to love, to love me?

Why were my nights spent cold and alone

while so many others basked by the hearth of love's fire?

Those painful memories melted away as I stroked your soft hair.

My lips pressing against you in a soft, slow kiss that lingered wonderfully.

Finally, love had found me ... after a life spent longing.

Your peaceful breathing calmed the restless winds of my soul, the angst that had permeated so many of my loneliest nights.

Indeed, every exhale from your beautiful lips seemed to be the soothing breeze of a warm wind that caressed my spirit.

Suddenly, I was a master of words who could find none, for there are some moments that letters on paper will never do justice ... and as my hand slid along your supple skin, my heart sighed in the realization that this was, indeed, a picture of timeless love that a thousand words would never begin to describe.

A wordsmith with no words, yet immeasurably content.

As I watched your exquisite form rise and fall with serene calmness in my arms, I stopped searching for words and smiled, choosing instead to relish the beauty of the scene unfolded ...

Of just how perfect this was – this stolen moment of joy.

My happiness spread from a single smile to a complete contentment as I finally understood.

Mate of my soul, friend of my spirit, love of my heart, you gave substance to the words I could always find before ...

You showed me what all the descriptions I had so long dreamed about actually meant ... and felt like.

I knew at that moment what I had never previously grasped.

Instead of dazzling words that failed to have meaning, I would trade all those wonderful tales and poems for this experience instead:

A moment, a lifetime with a love meant for me that defied description because words alone would never suffice.

The best love stories are beyond the pages, for they are told by the heart ...

And in your embrace, I felt every story, song and sonnet all fused into that cocoon of our love.

Happily ever after begins in your heart and lasts beyond lifetimes in your soul.

As I kissed your lips, lingering inches away lost in your eyes, I finally understood the meaning of forever.

I Want to Set My Soul on Fire

I don't want a lackluster life or an ordinary love … I need so much more than that.

I want to burn with the intensity of red-hot passion or not at all …

Passion for life, love and all the things that fill my soul.

I want to experience everything in this life that can't be found in a book or seen on a screen.

I want to feel the grass between my toes as I close my eyes and the warm wind gusts through my hair.

I want to hear the sweet laughter of happy child nearby and the quiet whispers of lovers cuddled up.

I want to feel the wet nose of a cute puppy and the rain of a warm summer shower falling onto my face.

The sweet smell of a blooming spring day and the chirping of crickets on a muggy summer night … that's what I love … that's what my heart craves.

The dancing fireflies that light up the twilight on a cool fall day reminds me – this is why I am alive.

I yearn to taste the fiery singe of love's passionate kiss often and run my fingers across my partner's skin.

I don't care about the ordinary choices that occupy the time of everyone else ...

No, give me the intensity of living in the moment and leaving no act undone nor any words left unsaid.

Leave the boring, dull and commonplace for others, I need the moments that set my soul on fire.

My road will lead me into uncharted waters that others have missed and places that are off the beaten path.

I want to know those feelings and sensations that make me feel alive, every day.

I want to lie in wonder under the pallid glow of a waning moon; I want to plunge headfirst into the beautiful splendor of the night sky.

I want to kiss endlessly, love recklessly and live truthfully.

I won't have a bucket list because I'll have done everything that I have ever yearned to experience.

My legacy won't be one of possessions, things or valuables, but of feelings, memories and fulfilled dreams.

I'll be the smile you never forget, the courage you never doubt and the heart that you never stop believing in.

I'll never be just a spark, a flame or a light.

I'll be a wildfire that sets your life on fire.

To feel my essence is to experience the burning sensation of being alive ...

truly energized in a way that fills every day, every moment with vigor.

I want to leave this place in such a way that with my last breaths I can say,

"I gave this life everything."

With love in my heart, and wonder in my soul, I'll spend the rest of my days exploring everything this world has to offer.

That's a little slice of the magic I keep tucked away in my spirit and will never relinquish ...

And you're never too old to stop believing in magic.

Unquenchable passion and intense desire –
that's how I live my life and enjoy my days.

No stone unturned, no words left unspoken, no dream unchased.

I don't want ordinary, average or almost.

I want to burn in the fires of a red-hot love, each and every day ...

And I want it all with you.

Let's go lose ourselves in the endless passion of forever ...

Truly alive, happy and free.

When Our Lips Meet and Souls Connect, Nothing Else Matters

In that instant when our lips meet,
There ceases to be a me or you,
Only a "we" ...
without ending –
Two bodies without separation,
Two souls fused into one,
Two hearts beating singularly.
The air I breathe is ours,
This love we have found is without equal.
In this moment, when we meet,
Souls colliding, hearts unifying and spirits melting into one ...
Passions' reckoning unending,
The world dissipates and time stands still ...
The cocoon of our love tucking us away from all else –
Because in those stolen moments,
We are all that matters,
Our love is all that I know ...
All that I feel, need and want ... nothing else.
If my life and love held but a solitary truth –

It would have a name, a face, a meaning ...
It would,
always has been
and always will be ...
you.

Long Before I Ever Met You

She realized that he was different from the first glance.
The way he moved, the way he spoke,
The way his gaze penetrated her soul.
She was so used to explaining herself to all the men she'd loved before ...
She was stunned when he just understood her without a word said.
She didn't know what to say or how to act having her soul bared before a man ...
It was deathly frightening,
But it was beautiful in a way that eclipsed words.
Moreover, she didn't try to hide or pretend because she didn't have to.
He just got it, he accepted and appreciated her ... all of her ... and that was something she'd never known.
Unconditionally and devotedly.
She was so used to kissing all the frogs hoping for a prince that she was speechless to finally meet the one that she knew was meant to be hers.

She tried to deny the connection and guard her heart, but it was no use.

She had yearned for this moment, this love, for so long that she was dumbfounded as it had found her so unexpectedly ...

But without a shadow of a doubt, with complete and utter certainty,

She knew he was the one.

So familiar, she felt as though they had loved each other for countless lifetimes before ...

And perhaps they had.

She just had this feeling that she had always known him.

As she nestled into him, her heart sighed and her soul felt at ease for the first time in, well, ever.

"This is what home feels like," she thought as she looked up at him.

Her voice cracked as she whispered, their eyes meeting as she spoke.

"I missed you, long before I ever met you."

He smiled and kissed her forehead.

Stroking her hair, he spoke the words she had waited a lifetime to hear.

"I'm just sorry it took me so long to find you, but I'm here now. Let's enjoy the rest of forever. I love you."

She sighed and burrowed deeper into his chest.

This was worth waiting a hundred lifetimes for, and she would cherish every moment of their love story just the way she had always wanted to be loved.

Meant to be will always find a way,

Just as it had for her that one beautiful day.

I Never Knew Love Until I Was Loved by You

You were the beautiful disaster that found a wonderful connection in me.

We were the last line to every love story and the first verse in every love song.

Happily ever after and fairy tales didn't ever seem to know where to find either of us until we discovered each other.

Truth be told, we just kinda stumbled into each other and, well, the rest is history.

Our history.

Our love story.

Not the sort of romantic adventure that features perfect heroes and amazing times, but the real kind with outrageous laughter,

awkward mistakes and innocent innuendos.

We didn't fall in love, we fumbled, bumbled and stumbled our way into it.

Yet, I wouldn't change a verse in our version of love.

I don't know who stole the light from your soul, but I see its radiance fighting to return home.

Buried beneath the soulful expression that guards your beautiful eyes,

I see the passage hidden to where I belong ...

Your soul and mine, joined forever as one.

You've kept your magic stashed away for so very long, it's amazing that it dances for me so wonderfully now,

But then, that's the way love is supposed to be.

You shine so brightly that the stars in heaven are jealous and love me with such passion that sets my soul on fire.

You've set my heart ablaze and my spirit at ease,

And in your touch, I feel the excitement of love's desire and the calm of love's fulfillment.

I don't know what tomorrow will bring, but the dying rays of today will find me loving you.

Loving You Endlessly

I know we've had some hard times and been through some tough days,

But we're still here, fighting for each other,

With love in our hearts ... believing in us no matter how hard it may get.

There are days when we can't seem to get on the same page and that's okay ...

We still find a way to make it through.

I know it hasn't always been easy, but the best things in life are worth fighting for ...

Like us.

We have a once in a lifetime love story, and I believe in us.

There are going to be stormy days and we won't always see eye to eye, but as long as we keep love in our hearts, communicate and work together, we can always find our way.

Hand in hand, heart to heart and soul to soul,

We have a beautiful love that won't end.

So, as I stand in front of you, I'm just asking you to love me at my worst and celebrate me at my best, as I will do for you.

And we will keep going, keep loving and keep thriving.
No matter what happens or how hard it gets, know that I'll never give up on us or stop loving you.
Me, you and forever ...
That's the love story that will always be
The most wonderful one of all:
Ours.

When Our Faces Are Lined with Wrinkles from a Life Well Lived

I look at you every day and see my future,
Sometimes, the love I have for you overwhelms me,
And there's nothing more I want
Than to spend the rest of my days loving you.

I want to celebrate the milestones with you,
I want to live in the moment of our lives,
I want to soak in the beauty around us,
As our love envelopes us for always.

Many years from now, when our hair is gray,
And our faces are lined with wrinkles
From a life well lived with love and laughter,
I want to look at you and just smile.

Holding your hand and looking in your eyes,
I want to think back to the memories we made,
The love we shared and the life we enjoyed.
The times won't always be perfect …
But it will be beautiful as long as it's with you.

Love Is the Person You Miss When Surrounded by Friends

I could be in a room full of people,
with good times and happy moments,
Music, fun and laughter filling the air,
And I'd still miss you by my side.

No matter where life takes me,
Or the joy it brings to my heart,
Everything just feels incomplete,
Until I can share it all with you.

Surrounded by my family and friends,
Celebrating, enjoying and loving the moment
…
Unless you are by my side, holding my hand,
It just doesn't feel right.

I can't explain how very deeply we are connected,
But I can feel you across a room or miles away,
Something deeper than I've ever known,

Ties my heart and soul beautifully to yours.

Once, I swore never to need another,
To stand strong on my own, defiant and proud,
To never be beholden to my heart and feelings,
Until you came into my life and changed it all.

Now, in the blink of an eye from worlds apart,
You have become my everything,
My best friend, my lover, my soulmate, my heart,
And the one thing I could never
Live without is you, ever again.

You're the Person I Want to Come Home To

You're my person ...

The one I want to share everything with.

My hopes, my dreams, my fears, my victories.

I want to come home at the end of my days, wrap up in your arms and just breathe in the comfort of your love.

I want to sit across from you and just talk about my days and all the things in them.

My frustrations, my happiness, my sadness and my successes.

Whenever something happens in my life – good or bad – you're the one I can't wait to share it with.

Truthfully, I can't imagine life without you holding my hand and protecting my heart.

You're the one who excites me and calms me at the same time ...

My joy and my peace ...

You put my soul at ease when nothing else can.

I don't know what tomorrow may bring or what challenges life will throw at us, but so long as you're by my side,
There's nothing we can't make it through,
Together.
Me and you, forever and always.
That's what I think about when I fall asleep each night and my first thought upon rising every morning.
In your arms, by your side and in your heart ...
There's no place else I'd rather be,
For the rest of my life.

In a World Full of Wrongs, You Choose to Always See What Is Right

All my life, people were trying to make me conform to their standards of what was right and how I should be.

They tell you to be yourself and then judge you if they don't approve of your choices.

For so long, that's just how I thought everything and everyone would always be ...

Until I met you.

You didn't criticize my flaws; you celebrated my imperfections.

You saw the person that I stowed behind placid eyes and slowly began to win my trust ...

And eventually, my heart and soul.

You didn't push, force or overwhelm –

You just let me be myself and loved me for everything I was in a way that I'd never known.

In an instant, you changed the story of my life with a chapter I couldn't have seen coming.

I thought the world was full of the same people doing the same things thinking the same way

...

You proved me wrong, and I've never been happier to be incorrect in my life.

It's so much more than just love, too.

You accept me unconditionally – all my jagged edges and broken pieces. Without question or hesitation, you hug them tightly and make me realize that everything will be okay.

You've shown me that love isn't a word, it's a powerful feeling that escapes definition and changed my world, my heart and my mindset.

You love me in such a way that it empowers me to love myself, my life and my future with relentless optimism.

I've come to learn that the darkness will find every one of us at times, and what matters is how we persevere.

Taking your hand, I know that we will always make our way through it.

The good times and the bad, big things and little … they all exist in brighter colors because of the love you've showered me with.

You're patient with my disastrous days, understanding through my emotional moods and most of all, you're just there for me, whenever I need you to be.

The moment you walked into my life, I knew why it had never worked out with anyone else.

Thank you for being you.

There's no place I would rather be than right beside you,

For the rest of our lives.

The Best Love Makes You Better

When I met you, I thought I had it all worked out.

I knew where I was going and had everything under control ... or so I thought.

Truth is, I didn't even have a clue.

You turned right into left and upside down into right side up.

You made me want to be better ...

Not just for you, but for me as well.

For both of us, for our relationship, for our future.

You changed what I thought would make me happy and what made me smile.

We talk about nothing for hours and laugh about the silliest things.

Conversations about deep feelings and the hysterical kind of laughter that makes my side hurt from laughing so hard.

You showed me that being the best version of myself is what matters the most —

And what you truly loved about me.

You're my best friend who thinks my jokes are funny ... even when I know they're kinda cheesy.

You're my soulmate who walks beside me in our life, holding my hand every day

You're my lover who excites me with each kiss and scintillates my soul with every touch.

You're my daily reminder of how amazing life can truly be ...

When I wake up and see your face smiling at me, it just makes me realize –

You made me believe again ...

In magic, in love and in you.

I wouldn't change a thing.

I love us for all the things we've been, what we are now and what we will always be.

Most of all because you'll always be mine ...

Forever and always.

When All That Really Matters Is That You're Together

No matter where life has led us,
Through the challenges and struggles,
Across the world and through the storms,
We still found our way back home, together.

We didn't always know where we were headed
Or even what we were doing sometimes,
All that I care about is that I did it all
With you beside me, holding my hand.

We've had our fair share of ups and downs,
Happiness and sorrow, but that's just life.
We always cherished our love or each other,
And we truly loved faithfully and honestly.

We've celebrated the milestones with joy
And we've enjoyed the small moments of life
Never forgetting each and every day,
To love each other along the way.

So, as I look into your eyes and my heart smiles,
It's from a life spent by your side, in love,
Experiencing the best and worst
Holding the hand of my one true love ...

My best friend, my lover, my soulmate and truth,
You've given me a lifetime of memories
And a heart full of love, and I smile.
I did it all with the best thing that's ever happened to me:
You.

Here's to many more, my love.

Moments Like These

When the still of the night is upon us,
And the serenity wraps us in its embrace,
As I watch your sleeping form
Nestled up to me, I couldn't ask for more.

In those moments, the world melts away,
And the cares and concerns of the day
Don't seem to matter anymore,
As I can think only of our love and you.

These are the times that I wish I could freeze,
Suspend time as we linger in love's grasp,
The quiet and still calming our hearts
As we are two souls connected as one.

All the thoughts, feelings and emotions
Just seemed to dissolve as we rest quietly,
Your motionless body next to mine,
My heart is full as I enjoy the beauty of the moment.

It's the snapshots of these instants

That I'll look back on and always remember,
For these are the memories of our life
That will always mean everything to me ...
Forever and always, yours.

One Moment Can Change Your Life, One Love Can Change Your World

From the very first moment, we knew.
It wasn't just the things we said or did,
It was what we didn't have to say or do.
It's what we just knew.
When you belong with someone,
Every fiber of your being aches to be with them.
From the first hello, that sense of belonging became much more than a thought, a desire or a need ...
It became a necessity.
I often used to wonder how I'd know or what it would feel like,
but the truth is, I can't describe the beauty and amazing feeling you have when you find the one meant for you.
Words fail the wonder of that feeling, it eclipses all description and lies beyond any understanding ...

Because I just knew ... and the power of the truth lies far beyond anything words could describe.

I knew the answer before I could even ask the question, and while that may not make sense to all, the ones who have been there will understand.

The glances that become conversations,

The kisses that become fire,

The moments that become memories.

There are countless ways that I love you and countless more reasons that I'm proud to be by your side.

I'll never let a day go by without reminding you how very much you're loved nor a time pass by where I don't show my appreciation ...

And most of all, I can't wait to build a home, a life and a future with you ...

Always and forever, my love.

Soulfully in Sync

I want more than superficial love ...

I need the deep, soulful connection that makes my heart sigh.

I've had ordinary desire and temporary longing; I'm done settling for those skin-deep feelings.

If it doesn't stir my soul, enflame my heart and fill my spirit with butterflies, then that's not my kind of love.

Don't get me wrong, I still want animal attraction, passionate fire and intimate closeness ... but I don't want just that ...

I need so much more than simple pleasures.

I crave it all ... and I will accept nothing less.

Let's do all the things that stimulate our mental connection – lie in bed reading to each other, have deep talks for hours about everything and nothing, lose ourselves in each other's minds deeply and intimately.

Maybe I'm a dreamer and holding out for the impossible, but it's what I want and deserve.

Let's set the night on fire with the chain reaction of our love story – from the mind to the soul to everything else – that transcends the normalcy of the ordinary.

Stimulate my mind, connect with my soul, set my heart on fire so that even the smallest touch electrifies our skin.

I've waited a lifetime to find this sort of love, and until you found me, I didn't know what all that meant ... it was all just wishes and wants.

You've made it more than real; you've transformed my life into the love story I had long dreamt of.

I always knew what I wanted in life and love, but you came into my world and made it all real.

You've made your heart into my home, your arms where I belong and the future beautiful by your side.

Everything's better when it's shared with someone you love.

Thank you for making all the dead ends and broken roads worth every wrong turn and bad decision.

I couldn't have dreamt that I would find everything I had ever wanted in you.

In the middle of an ordinary life, you gave me a fairytale.

Our Souls Are the Same

From the very first moment, we knew.

We'd both heard all the stories and knew all the ways love was supposed to feel, but until you come face to face with that indescribable moment when you just know that they're the one, it's all just pretty words.

But in that magical moment when you know, everything changes ... your hopes, dreams and even where you want to be.

All I could think of was you ... being beside you, in your arms, holding you close, building a future together.

It's almost unbelievable when you find yourself saying the same things at the same times, liking the same weird things or just sharing a powerful connection that can't be denied.

I'd always heard others talking about that intimate closeness that two people can share, but like most, I brushed it off as fairytale nonsense.

And then I met you.

You changed everything I thought I knew about love, and I've never been so happy to be utterly wrong.

We're the same, you and I, and always have been.

In all the big, beautiful ways and even the little gorgeous ways too.

Where I stop and you start, I'll never know — nor do I want to.

There are a lot of things I don't know about this life, but I do know this:

You've been mine since before we ever met, even when you were just a dream.

Since you found me, everything has changed, and I never want to go back to the way things used to be.

With you is where I belong.

In my arms, in my heart and forever in love.

You Will Forever Be My Always

You asked me how I knew that I loved you.
You wondered why I chose you.
Honestly?
I didn't choose you.
My heart fell in love with yours.
Our souls connected in a way I'd never known.
I saw it in your eyes, felt it in your touch.
Butterflies made room for physical cravings –
to hold you, to be close to you.
When I was away from you, every fiber of my being longed to be in your arms again.
Those feelings – emotional, physical and soulful – redefined everything I ever thought I knew about love.
You were the missing piece, the safe place, the beautiful truth I had always searched for.
In that moment, when your lips touched mine for the very first time, it was more than a feeling or an emotion.
It was meant to be.

When I kissed your lips and realized how wrong every other kiss had ever been, it was then that I more than knew.

The answer that I had long sought showed up just when it was meant to, not a moment sooner.

I look in your beautiful eyes and see the reflections of my soul, and I know all the reasons why I fell for you.

And I'll spend the rest of my days reminding you of all the ways you're beloved to me.

My love for you can't be described in any words I've ever known,

And I can't verbalize forever in a way that doesn't pale in comparison to the beautiful love that I found in you.

I love you, for you will forever be my always.

The Heart Knows When the Search Is Over

All her life, she had searched the world over,
Longing for love and hoping to find her happily ever after.
She turned over every stone, kissed every frog,
Looked around each corner ... to no avail.

Possibly slowly turned into never,
All the hopes she once had seemed
To vanish with bad choices and even worse men.
She fretted as she wondered if "he" truly existed.
She started to think fairytales didn't come true.

It was on a beautiful Sunday afternoon,
Out of nowhere and in a way completely
Unexpected, unbelievable and unanticipated,
She came face to face with a man who seemed ... familiar.

His gaze met hers, their souls found one another,
And in an instant, she experienced a calm never before known.
His voice soothed her spirit,
His touch felt like home.

All the doubts and insecurities melted away,
As if they had never even existed.
Her "nevers" transformed into "always"
Her "not nows" changed into "forever."

She learned the hardest lesson of all:
Love comes in its own time and own way.
You can't predict it or even understand it.
All you can do is cherish it when it arrives.

For when Cupid's arrow finds your heart,
You'll recognize in an instant that they are the one ...
Your true love, your soulmate, your forever twin flame.
She smiled – she had finally kissed her last frog.

In the middle of an ordinary life, she had found a fairytale.

Afraid of the Realness

I'm scared, just like you are.

I've never experienced anything like our love before, not ever, not in any way.

Our connection is so powerful that I can't explain how I feel, only that it's something I've become sure of – like the sun rising or being able to breathe.

I know you've never found someone you couldn't live without before,

And that terrifies you.

You don't like the trust you're surrendering or the vulnerability this creates between us.

I'm right there with you.

I never expected to find you. I never believed that feelings of this magnitude even existed.

You've been hurt before, and I know your heart can be fragile.

I also know that building the right foundation will take time, patience and love ...

And I'm prepared to do whatever it takes to protect your heart and show you that I'm for real.

It's crazy really, how our lives collided into love.

We were two people content and living our best lives solo ... until this love story knocked on our doors and changed everything.

I didn't expect it, I still don't know what to make of it sometimes, but I'm embracing you, our love and our future with open arms.

So, we don't need to rush. Let's just walk for a while and get to know each other ...

Let's learn the language of our hearts, explore the connection of our souls, and truly dive deeper into this amazing gift that we've been blessed with.

I can't promise I'll always be perfect or that life will be easy, but if we work together, hold hands through the hard times and never stop loving each other openly and honestly, there's nothing we can't do ... together.

I've waited my whole life for you, so let's just build our trust, our lives and our future, one day at a time.

This is really happening, so let's pinch ourselves every so often and remind each other how much we love each other, every day in every way.

Scared, happy, excited, worried, blissful ...

All the things we both feel are normal and natural.

Let's just make sure that we do whatever we can ...

To communicate, to work together and to fall in love with each other all over again,

Every day.

My heart and soul will always be entwined and in love with yours ...

Forever starts today.

And I Choose You

From worlds apart and miles away,
We found each other against all odds.
Love was never in our sights,
But it was intent on uniting you and me.

We were content in our lives,
Chasing our dreams the best we could ...
Only we never knew that we were missing
That connection we found in us.

From the first word, the first laugh,
The very first moment we knew,
Everything changed in us and our lives.
We suddenly needed something never known:
Each other.

I can't say I've ever felt a power like this,
A hunger for your love like I know now,
Only that I'm incomplete without you,
Needing you every day in every way.

In that singular moment when I found you,
It all changed when you became my everything.
Nothing would ever be the same,
Nor would I want it to be.

You're my happy place at day's end,
The kiss that welcomes me home,
A burning to be in your arms,
That eclipses the need for all else.

So, as we embrace and the world melts away,
Know that it is these moments I treasure,
Our love suspended in beautiful bliss ...
Soulmates, best friends, twin flames, partners ...
Forever and always, 'til time is no more.

She Was a Warm Embrace, His Reminder of Beauty in the World

No matter how hard life could be, she was always waiting for him, arms open –

The warm embrace at the end of a sometimes-cold day, reminding him that his safe place was forever in his arms.

Though they parted every morning to pursue their various endeavors, they never lost their beautiful connection, for they always carried their love with them, no matter how far they traveled.

A simple text, quick call or little nudges of love between them always kept their fire burning when the world tried to quench the spark.

There were always moments when life brought them to their knees, but together, hand in hand, they always found their way and their strength to push forward ...

Never losing their special bond, for that was the essence of their souls.

They both knew that she was his fire, and he was her rock, and their hearts beat as one, even as the world could come crashing down around them.

In a life that did everything to tear them apart and destroy their love, they always found each other and nurtured the beauty of their connection, each and every day.

Maybe it wasn't perfect or full of grandiose moments, but it was real, it was true, and more than anything,

It was the two of them, loving each other in their own special way.

Some of our love stories may be a little dented and scratched, but they're every bit as beautiful as the fairytales.

Because they're our own special love, told in a beautiful way that only we will know and appreciate.

And that's the most wonderful part of all.

I Would Wait for You Forever

I never meant to fall in love with you, but when I saw you, I never stood a chance.

You smiled and stole my heart before I realized I had fallen for you.

I never really stood a chance, but then, I didn't really want to.

You blew in like a whirlwind and ripped my defenses asunder, and I was yours – with a beautiful smile and a sumptuous kiss.

Loving you wasn't even an option, because when your soul called to mine across a windswept plane, I fell completely head over heels for you.

Your words careened across my skin with precocious splendor,

And your lips upon mine seduced me with a fiery passion that I have never known.

As the days have passed and our hearts have begun to beat as one,

I realized more and more how very familiar you've always been to me.

We were never strangers from the moment we met,

We just hadn't found each other yet in this lifetime.

I knew when I looked in your eyes that our love was timeless – without beginning or end.

Mate of my soul, you have been my twin flame since before the chapters of time ever turned the first page.

Head to heart to spirit to soul, we've loved each other across countless times and endless places.

Against impossible odds, we've always found our way back to each other's arms.

Our love has endured when all else failed,

Your touch has always electrified my senses and calmed my restless spirit.

More than just butterflies and sweet whispers,

You've been my reason for being and my light in the darkness.

I'll hold your hand in mine as we face the world and years together,

And I'll find you once more in the next life …

Even if I have to wait a hundred years to love you again,

I'd count the minutes until you were there,

Knowing that my forever begins and ends …

With you.

I'd gladly wait for a hundred years if it meant you would find me at the end.

Each and every time.

That's love.

That's true.

That's us.

We are and always will be forever in love.

Show Me Your Truth and Then Let Me Love You

Darling, come experience this life with me in the wildest and most amazing ways we can find.

Leave behind all the worldly stuff and let's just be us for a while ... no, change that ... not just for a time, but for forever.

Kiss me in the rain and hold my hand as we dance through the puddles of life ...

Don't let me go, ever – no matter how hard the storms come.

Turn up the music we love and let's pretend like we're giving the concert of our lives ...

Let's sing at the top of our lungs and not care who is watching or listening ...

This is our life and our love; we don't need anyone's permission or approval to be our silliest selves and love each other in just the ways we want.

In truth, that's what I want from you, all the time in all the ways.

Show me who you really are – bare your soul to mine so that we will never lose that connection that makes our love so special.

Tell me the truth, even when I don't want to hear it ... because that's what you'll always get from me.

Sure, I'm human, and I'm going to make mistakes – we both will ...

But that doesn't change how we feel or the love we have ... it just makes our love stronger through the ups and downs.

So, take my hand and let's do all the things the world says we shouldn't.

Road trips to nowhere for no reason other than to just enjoy each other.

Laying in a field under a star-filled sky, holding hands and talking for hours.

Rainy days with the music turned up full blast so that we can dance throughout the house ...

In the kitchen, living room or on the patio outside – let the moonlight serenade our love.

Because Darling, we are one of a kind and meant to be, and there's no force on earth that can keep our love from blossoming.

So, let's lose ourselves in the life, the love and the laughter that fills our souls.

I've waited my whole life to hold your hand in the rain ...

We might as well dance in it while we're here.

Kiss Her as if You are Writing Poetry on Her Soul

Would your lips tremble if I kissed them?
Would your heart melt if I ignited your passion?
Would your soul long for mine if I called out for you?
Would your love be mine if I chose you, ever after?
As the hands of time edge tenuously forward,
I hold everything in my arms
As I look at you.
I don't know how I found you or why I am so blessed,
only that I look at you daily and wonder how
Such a beautiful love could enrapture me.
So, as I take your soft face into my hands,
drinking in your soulful eyes,
I wonder so many things,
but most of all, this:
If I fall into the madness of your love,
plunge headfirst into the depths of your heart,
will you catch me and keep me, forevermore?
It's a chance I'm willing to take.

Here and Where You Are

No matter where I am or the day I've had,
My heart and soul are always with you.
Miles apart or beside each other,
I'm always there, holding your heart.

We found each other against impossible odds,
Worlds apart and a chance somehow found,
You've given my heart a home,
And my soul a companion for always.

The very moment we lose ourselves in embrace,
Time slows and the world dissipates
As we seek refuge in our hidden place,
Our cocoon of surreal love and peace.

You've had me since the very first moment
When our eyes met and souls collided,
And I knew in that instant,
I'd finally found my forever in you.

I know that we've had our ups and downs,

Tragedies and triumphs will always be,
But together, we can weather any storm,
And our love will always see us through.

So, as our days carry us to places apart,
Know that I will carry your love with me,
Tucked away in the safety of my heart,
And forever will you be ...
Beautiful in my eyes.

I Choose Both

I know there's just going to be those days that you just can't get it together, because I have them too.

When you're running late, wearing mismatched socks and forgot to eat as you're bounding off to your day, and that's just life sometimes.

I don't expect you to be perfect because I'm far from it.

In fact, what makes us perfect for each other is how wonderfully all our jagged edges fit together.

There will be days you need my strength and other times when I'll need your positivity, but that's what will carry us through the hard times.

Things won't always go as planned, but as long as we can depend on each other, we will find our way through.

I've celebrated your victories on your best days and I've held your hand during the hard times … I've seen your best and your worst, and I choose both, for always.

I'll have my moods and you'll have your days too, but if we stick together and remember what's important,

There's nothing we can't do together.

True love isn't about just being happy during the easy times and good days, it's about standing strong through all the days, both good and bad.

It won't always be easy, in fact it may be rocky sometimes, but so long as we have love in our hearts and hope in our spirits –

You, me and us –

We will always be better together than apart,

And we always will be,

This I promise you.

Every Time I Follow My Heart It Leads Me to You

I've spent a lot of my life making wishes on stars,

Hoping that love would find me sooner rather than later.

I've gone down a lot of broken roads and tried to make partners out of projects,

And all those relationships ended in heartache … until I met you.

You were everything I never knew I needed until you showed me how amazing love could be.

You loved me at my worst and celebrated me at my best, holding my heart and hand through it all.

Our love did more than fulfill me, it made me want to be a better person – for me, for you, and for us.

You're my refuge from any storm and my happy place at the end of a day,

For you've shown me what love can truly be.

So, every time I smile when your name pops up on my phone, it's because you've changed my heart, my love and most of all, my life.

Every day, in every way ... when I'm greeted by your beautiful face,

I can't help but fall head over heels for you all over again ...

After all, isn't that what a real love story is all about?

Falling in love is at the heart of every happily ever after ...

That's just what I plan to do, with you, for the rest of our lives together ...

Fall in love all over again, every day,

Now and for always.

Your Love Feels Like Sunshine

When you found me, I thought I knew love.
I believed I understood what love meant,
How it really felt and how it was to go ...
How wrong I was in all those thoughts.

You showed me feelings that I had never known,
In ways I'd never imagined,
In truths I couldn't have understood,
When you gave me your heart.

The contentment in your arms,
The fire in your desire,
The love in your eyes
The ferocity of your passion ...
All beautiful parts of you that I'll always treasure.

Those feelings were just the door creaking open
To a cascading flood of the wonders of you,
That your heart, your love and your soul

Showed me from the very first time we touched.

You didn't just make me feel loved,
You helped me learn how to love myself,
Held my hand through the struggles,
And wiped away my tears during the pain.

I'll never know how I came to be so blessed when I found you,
Only that I drift off every night and wake each morn,
With a happiness in my soul that you brought to me,
A light in my heart that beats stronger for you.

Come what may, no matter where life leads us,
I'll walk the path with you by my side,
Thankful, hopeful and blissful,
As plainly as the sun's warmth above,
Loving you, for the rest of our lives.

Wild and Free

She was the free spirit that lived without the need of anyone's permission or acceptance.

She had always been all the things no one ever understood, and she was okay with that.

An old soul, empathetic and wild, she made no excuses for who she was and how she lived.

She lived in the moments of her life, reveling in the beauty all around her and losing herself in the wonders that she beheld.

She believed deeply in the things most people had forgotten or overlooked: passionate love, soul depth and fiery desire.

Her life was almost perfect, it seemed ...

Until she met him.

He showed her how to be more than just wild, but how to spread her wings and truly fly.

His love and appreciation for all the things that she cherished most about herself empowered her in such a way that she found a newfound courage in the possibilities that she had once avoided.

It was one thing to be wild, yet another to be free.

Their love elevated her wild beauty to a level she had never known, and she loved him fiercely for who she was with him.

He was everything she never knew she needed but now craved intensely ...

Respect, empowerment ... the click they felt was unlike anything she'd ever known.

He just got her in a way no one else ever had.

From across a room or even miles away, he just had an uncanny way of sensing her energy and being there for her – sometimes, when she didn't even know she needed him to be.

She had never looked for a man to complete her, but when his love took hold of her heart, she found everything about herself and her life became that much better.

Most of the time, she couldn't explain how he had enriched her life, only that their love was something long ago written in the stars,

A destiny that she knew was always meant to be.

No matter how high she flew or the challenges that faced her, she now attacked her life with a fiery spirit that would not be denied ... the fears from the past just seemed to melt away.

Before she met him, she was always wild, strong and beautiful ...

Now, she was so much more than that ...

He had helped her see the way to be something greater and stronger ...

Now, she was finally free.

One Person Can Show You That All People Are Not the Same

I realize that when I see the hurt behind your eyes, I'm only uncovering a very small part of your story.

Your gaze speaks volumes, and the whisper of your soul utters a thousand words I will never forget.

Yet, I know that I've only seen a glimpse of the person who lies hidden beneath the surface.

You've protected your heart because of all the ones in your past who tried to do more than hurt you, they wanted to control who you were.

The weak will always seek to reduce and diminish the strong, but you were better than that, smarter than them.

They never really got close enough to the soul behind the mask to take away your identity or break your spirit.

But it's made you so very cautious and hesitant to seek love again, and rightly so.

They hurt you because, deep down, you wanted to believe that they were different.

But until someone comes along who sees past the facade, behind your walls and through to your soul, all the others will always be the same ...

Until me.

I know you don't need to be saved, completed or fulfilled.

You simply long to be loved, respected and appreciated for the person you are, the road you've traveled and the person you've worked hard to become.

But to truly comprehend the depths of you, it takes more than a day, week or a month:

It takes a lifetime ...

And I'm willing to dive deeply into your truths and unravel the secrets you've tucked away ...

However long it takes.

Each level of your hidden beauty unveiled only gives way to a deeper and more wondrous truth.

You've been waiting a long time to reveal who you really are to someone,

even longer to trust someone with every aspect of your heart.

I'm willing to be as patient as it takes, to slowly help you take down your walls to reveal the most precious parts of your heart ...

You're worth that and so very much more to me ...

Truth is, I've searched all my life for the person who my soul would recognize in the passing of a second.

You're my soul mate – my person, who I've known since before I knew of anything else –

I just hadn't found you yet in this lifetime.

I wish your broken road hadn't hurt you,

I wish that all the ones before weren't lessons,

but as our paths were always meant to converge, I know now that this was always the road we were meant to travel.

It hasn't been easy, there will always be hard days, but it will all be worth it in the end.

After all, once in a lifetime is worth any road, no matter how long or broken.

One man, one woman, one love.

Your smile and embrace tell me that you finally feel the one thing the others never could make you feel:

Safe.

As I look in your eyes, I can feel my heart smile as the single thought comes to me.
I've finally found where I belong, in this life, with you.

Already Fallen

Our meeting was never simply chance,
We were always meant to be.
The universe conspired to create our love,
A union since long forged in the stars above.
Across countless times and lifetimes past,
Our souls have always found each other,
Regardless of the distance or struggle.
We always have and will be together in love.
You became the dream that filled my nights,
The face without a name before ever meeting,
I knew of you intimately before our souls collided,
You were always meant to be my true love.
As I lose myself in your eyes tonight,
A glimmer of love and lives past rekindles
And my heart stirs as I remember us from before.
Soulmates, twin flames and true love.
In your smile, I see the warmth that I have missed,
In your arms, the embrace that calls me home,
In your laugh, the sweet serenade of your love,

And in your kiss,
The reminder of our never-ending love story,
Evermore.

When I Still Tasted Like Heartbreak

When you found me, I was an utter mess –
Completely broken and without joy.

I wasn't much fun to be around, and I couldn't see through my darkness.

I had lost the joy of living and couldn't dig my way out of the hole of loss and anguish I had buried myself in.

But you showed me that love isn't full of just heartache and pain … that there's a different side of love that I had never felt before.

I know you've been here through it all, and I just wanted to say thank you.

You've been patient with my fragile heart and held my hand through the hard days …

Even wiped away my tears as I cried.

I thought heartache would destroy me, and it truly might have if you hadn't shown up when you did.

Your selfless love and undying devotion to my broken soul started to show me how to let the light in again.

You loved me when I didn't love myself and showed me kindness without expectation … something I had never known.

I'm sure I would have found my way eventually, but you led me from a place of love ...

And I don't think "thank you" will ever truly encompass how very deeply I care about you.

It's been a long journey with a lot of down days, but you've never backed down or disappeared a single time, though I'm sure it wasn't always easy ...

I was a disaster for the longest time … and not the beautiful sort.

You didn't just help me put the pieces of my broken self back together, you held my hand as you patiently showed me the way back to myself.

You reminded me of my strength when I didn't have the courage to look for it myself.

I couldn't face the demons that haunted my thoughts at night, but you danced with them, distracting them in a way that somehow gave me peace … if only for a time.

So, as I look into the eyes of your beautiful soul, I'm overwhelmed with the blessing that I found in you.

You were everything I never knew I needed, and you gave me a safe haven from my storms.

You loved me when I didn't know how to love myself,

And for that and so much more,

I'm going to spend the rest of our lives showing you just how very special you are to me.

Thank you for being here through it all, loving me unconditionally,

And most of all, showing me how to love myself when I had forgotten how.

You're my one true thing,

Now and for always.

There Are Not Enough Stars

I always longed to find the person who would fall in love with my smile,

the one would adore me even when I snorted and cackled when I laughed.

Many times, I thought I had found true love ... only to be left holding the pieces of my broken heart.

The fall from love was infinitely harder than falling into it.

And soon, you start to lose hope that you'll ever really find your person.

The "one" seemed impossible to find as my efforts to seek love always ended in failure.

I couldn't solve the riddle of the heart until,

In the blink of an eye, you changed everything for me.

All the others never really saw me for me until you glimpsed into my soul the very first time we met ...

The real, goofy and deep person I was didn't scare you like it did the ones before you.

In fact, it only drew you closer to me, and slowly, you started tearing down the walls around my heart.

I watched you smile and laugh with me every day,

and soon, it became very clear –

the epiphany of my love's journey was right in front of me.

You loved me for me – honest and real, without judgement or conditions.

Tears flooded my eyes as awe struck my heart.

How did you see what all the others had missed?

You engaged my mind, stoked my passions and whispered to my soul.

All along, it was always meant to be you ...

I knew you were the one from our very first smile,

I felt you were the one from our very first embrace.

You gave rhyme to my reason and hope to my tomorrows.

You were my one wish once made on a shooting star,

Dreaming that a love like yours could ever find me in a world full of broken roads and shattered hearts.

Truth be told, I'd say I could use the stars to count the ways that I love you,

But then, I'd run out of stars.

So, until they create a word that combines all the amazing and wondrous things that encompass my feelings for you,

I'll just stick with three.

I love you.

That's the best start to a life together and a better love story than I could have ever imagined.

Me and you, for always.

There's nowhere else I'd rather be

Than in your arms, for the rest of our days.

Finding the Small Miracles Among the Ordinary

I want to do all the things I've never done with you by my side.

I want to roll the windows down and let the wind blow through my hair.

I want to turn the music up and feel it permeate my soul as we chase adventure in obscure places and enjoy the beautiful serenity of peaceful retreats.

Let's soak in the wonder of those moments when we find the open road, a forest trail or hidden alcove where our dreams can come alive.

Let's hide away, if only for a bit, and escape the commotion of life.

I want to take in the history of places we've never been, enrich my mind in ways I've never done and always keep growing, learning and evolving.

I know there will days when I'll be a feisty handful and a complete mess, but that's just part of my unique charm ...

Or at least that's what I'm going with.

Those are the days I just need you to hold my hand and feed me chocolate.

It won't solve any problems, but it will make me feel better when I need it most.

You'll won't always know why I'm upset or even the reasons why I'm in a tizzy, but you don't have to.

I don't even understand myself sometimes – but those are the times I need you to love me hardest ... when I'm struggling.

Let's steal away moments at night when the world is slumbering to enjoy the quiet of our time together.

Relaxing in a tub while you read aloud our favorite love story will always be one of my most treasured memories,

The times where we leave the world behind and connect ... your soul and mine.

I want to live each day to its fullest, finding the small miracles among the ordinary that make our hearts smile.

Let's turn our faces to the sunlight and leave the wind at our backs, experiencing the joys that challenge our minds, fill our hearts and enrich our souls.

Forget the ordinary – I want out of the labels, the boxes and expectations of who I should be …

Let's redefine ourselves and discover what makes us feel extraordinary.

I want more than to just exist, let's fall in love with being alive every day.

We will always have time to rest, spending those days wrapped up in the cocoon of our loving embrace …

So, when life gives us the chance to chase our dreams and live in the moment, let's seize those opportunities with relentless optimism and reckless abandon.

We never know what tomorrow will bring, so let's enjoy today for the wonderful gift that it is …

Let's love with zealous passion, live with fierce purpose and always follow our hearts.

You, me and forever … we will always be truly alive just past the horizon to our dreams.

The Enchanting Cocoon of Your Loving Embrace

There's just something beautiful about the moment when I first reach your arms.

As your arms wrap around me for a warm embrace, time slows and the world melts away.

No matter the day I've had nor the struggles I've endured, everything just seems right in those moments.

Honestly, if I could stay forever in your arms, I'd probably never leave the enchanting cocoon of your loving embrace.

The feelings that we exchange through those simple but powerful moments almost escape words, because it feels so amazing as I soak in your touch … your love … your soul.

They say it's the big moments that define our lives, but it's the little memories of being in your arms that will always linger in my mind and heart.

There's nothing I would ever change about us, except maybe that we could stay in each other's arms, forever.

There's no place I'd rather be than in your heart and arms, for always.

I Didn't Know What to Wish for … Until You

There was a time that seems so long ago,
That I didn't think love would ever find me.
Wishing on shooting stars, always hoping,
That someday, destiny would come calling.

I really didn't know what I wanted,
Other than the cliches that I had heard,
Because until real and lasting love finds you,
You don't know how powerful it truly is.

All the dreams and hopes I once had,
The ideals and desires melted away
Once your smile brightened my life,
And I realized that all I knew was wrong.

You showed me the true meaning of love,
How amazing life could be when you find
The one meant to be yours,
And forever takes on a completely new
meaning.

I never could have imagined the love I found in you,
Nor the way you leave me breathless,
As you embrace me with a powerful love
That engulfs me and never lets me go.

And while I didn't know your name or face,
I now realize what I had known all along ...
It was always you that was meant for me,
As it will always be us, two that became one –

For my love story has finally smiled at me,
Bringing us to a place we shall never leave.
Until time is no more and forever ceases to be,
I'll always be loving you, endlessly.

Once in a While, Love Gives Us a Fairy Tale

In the fairy tales, it always goes the same:
Princess saved by the knight in shining armor
… they find white picket fences and a cozy cottage and live happily ever after.
All my life, that's how I thought it was supposed to be.
That's just how I imagined true love stories happened.
I tried to save those who would not be saved and ended up with nothing but heartache.
I chased others that weren't worth catching and tried to love those who would not be loved.
I spent nights dreaming of my love
and days hoping with always the same result: loneliness.
I'd hold onto that desire and close my eyes whenever the chance arose … crossing my fingers that love would come calling.
It was never meant to be … until I found the right one.
Around every corner, I'd hold my breath,

Hoping a wonderful smile would greet me just beyond.

Maybe, just maybe, the love of my dreams just wasn't real, that I wasn't meant to be part of a "we."

Always the same result.

Always empty wishes and dead end hopes.

Days turn to months and months dragged into a blur.

I tried not to give up hope.

I wanted to believe that there's someone out there for all of us, including me.

I fought to believe that dreams come true and that my hopes would not be in vain.

Despair slowly crept into my days and angst deeper into my nights.

My wish had expired, it had seemed, and the light of my once promising dreams of love was fading.

Until …

One summer day, my head buried in my music,

Melancholy permeating my mind until suddenly,

Someone shook me out of my musical trance.

Opening my eyes, I discovered an amazing smile staring back at me.

She pulled the earphone from my ear, introduced herself and remarked that she couldn't help but overhear my music ...

She wondered why I seemed sad, because I had a kind face.

Losing myself in those rueful hazel eyes, an epiphany sparked.

I had it wrong all along.

Maybe it wasn't always about the knight in shining armor saving the princess.

Maybe, just maybe, sometimes it's an amazing princess rescuing a wayward knight.

As we talked and walked, something inside of me changed.

It wasn't about who needed saving or being something I wasn't,

It was about accepting whatever version of my love story showed up.

As I looked over at her beaming smile, I knew that the rules didn't matter and the details weren't important.

Two people, one soul, a beautiful ending to the happiest story that I could have imagined.

I didn't know how to write the opening chapters of my life, but now, I know how the story ends.

Life has a funny way of showing you a different way of thinking you never expected.

It all started with a smile … and ended with forever.

Once in a while, in the middle of an ordinary life, love gives us a fairy tale.

Stand Under the Stars with Me Forever

I don't need fancy promises of grandiose things or expensive possessions.

Material gifts and tangible trappings are quite nice – don't get me wrong –

but they're not what fuels our dreams and gives life to our hopes ...

Certainly not what enriches true love ...

Our love.

Promises to visit faraway lands and the best that money can buy will never be what I want from you.

All that I want, for now and always, is just you.

The best things in life are and always will be free ... your love, greatest of all.

Your best days, your worst times and all the other ones squeezed in the middle –

facing them all by my side.

Kisses in the rain, hands held in the still of night are what makes my heart beat wildly for you.

The feeling of contentment of heart and soul will always make me sigh when we touch.

The look in your eye that draws me in and the smile that melts my heart –
that's why I will walk beside you until we can walk no more.
Our victories and our defeats,
tragedies and triumphs ...
It only makes our love that much more beautiful.
Our small memories and our grand accomplishments spark my spirit in ways I've never known.
Even the stormiest days followed by the brightest nights ...
These are all I want with you, side by side, taking on the world.
I don't need promises of things to make me happy.
It's pretty simple, really.
I just need you.
There's nothing else I could ever want ...
especially when I'm holding everything in my arms when I'm pulling you to me.
Falling asleep beside you is the waking dream I've waited a lifetime for ... and I would wait countless more if I had to.

It was always you and it always will be ...

You complete me in a way I never thought possible.

You and I have something special ...

Our happily ever after written in a style distinctly our own.

There's no place I'd rather be than in your arms, totally in love with you.

Forever and always, that's where I'll be.

Waiting for you, on the steps to love forevermore.

Look for Someone Who Won't Let You Face the World Alone

When life brings you to your knees,
And you don't know where my turn,
As your hope fades like the last sunlight,
Know that I'll always be there for you.

I can't solve your problems
Nor do I have all the answers,
But I'm here to stand beside you
And always listen when you need it most.

There will always be storms,
And the times that threaten to tear us apart,
But hand in hand, side by side,
We can weather anything with love in our hearts.

I'll be the first to embrace you after a long day,
Welcoming you home to my loving arms,
Kissing your forehead and stroking your hair,
Telling you it's all going to be okay.

Since we've met, we've never been apart,
For your heart is my home,
Your love is my refuge from life,
Our hidden haven from the world around.

Two hearts that found each other
When we needed it most.
Brought together for the most intimate reason,
For a true love like ours will
Always find its way.

We Fall in Love by Chance, We Stay in Love by Choice

Darling,
When I fell in love with you,
I didn't know anything could feel this wonderful
... every time I get lost in your eyes,
I know how incomplete I was before I met you.
I never realized how amazing love could truly feel ...
How one person could elicit such intense passion while soothing my spirit at the same time.
That was a feeling I never could have imagined until you made it real.
But now that I do, I'll be planning to spend the rest of my life choosing each and every day ...
To fall in love with you, all over again ...
Two hearts entwined, wrapped in love's embrace until time is no more.
From the first glance I ever saw you until the horizon meets the sky,
We will always be my favorite love story.

Life Needs More Slow Dances, Stolen Kisses and Quiet Moments

My Love,

Let's stop time for a bit and lose ourselves in the moments –

Our frozen cocoon of love that will melt the world away as we simply enjoy our love story for a long and wonderful rendezvous.

Let's slow dance wherever we are,

Let's slow kiss whenever we can,

And let's just slow down and love each other as often as we should.

Let's never let life stop us from stealing away from the world and reclaiming our passionate love.

This is the magic that will keep us falling in love every day.

Kiss me deeply like every time is the first time

...

The last thought as I fall asleep each night and the first smile as I rise each morning,

That is my wish and promise to you,

For always.

Let's do more than just love each other respectfully, devotedly and passionately ...

Let's promise to always carve out the moments that we will transform into beautiful memories ...

Slow dances in the kitchen,

Stolen kisses in a hidden doorway,

Quiet moments of love that we will treasure throughout our years together.

Let's stoke the fires of our love,

One beautiful moment at a time ...

Forever in your arms,

until all fades away into love's embrace,

Evermore.

You Don't Want the Stars, so I'll Bring You the Ocean Instead

When you came into my life,
All you wanted was love and respect.
You didn't ask for fancy dinners and expensive gifts.
You needed someone to see you for who you truly are and always would be.
The others before me had never really understood the magic of your soul.
They looked past the things that mattered to find the things they wanted.
That wasn't love, it was selfish.
You'd never been appreciated and respected the way you deserved.
You'd been holding out for a hero and all you got was a narcissistic zero.
They didn't love you … they loved what they wanted you to be.
Love is unselfish, it is kind, it is compassionate and so many things that you've never found before.

So, you may not ask for the sun, moon and stars, and though you deserve so much more than that, let's start with something every day.

Falling in love.

Being kind and considerate.

Always being thoughtful and respectful.

Communicating and being there for each other, through the tragedies and triumphs.

I'll dance with you in the rain and I'll hold you tightly through the storms.

There's nothing I won't do for you – this I promise, for now and always.

You didn't want the stars or moon, so I'll bring you the ocean instead ...

For every night as the water rushes in to find the shore,

So shall my love always be.

True and without fail,

Know that I loved you before I ever knew you ...

When you were just a thought and dream, you were always my love.

Sing to me the song of your heart, my love, and let's lose ourselves in the magic of our love story ...

For you are and always will be, my waking dream that finally came true.

You Have Me

From worlds apart against impossible odds,
Your heart found mine as destiny wove its magic,
Uniting our souls as was always meant to be,
The universe conspiring to create our love.

Unwavering, unbreakable and unending,
Our story transformed into a love
Unlike any we had ever known.
We had always believed against hope that we would find each other ...

As I hold your hand and gaze into your eyes,
Know that you are my everything –
Soulmate, best friend and lover,
A safe place more amazing than I could have imagined.

Until the last star in every galaxy burns out,
And the whisper of life breathes no more,
Know this one simple truth:
You have me –

now and forever ... and you always have.

You Did Something for Me I Couldn't Do for Myself. You Loved Me for Who I Am

There was a time when I didn't know how to love myself the way that I knew I should.

I believed all the worst things about myself and didn't know how to believe any of the best.

I knew that I would never truly be able love anyone else the way they deserved if I couldn't start with loving myself.

I didn't know where to start or when what to do, so I just threw myself into trying to believe I was good enough,

That I was truly worthy of love.

I frustratingly tried to fight and dig my way to a deeper understanding of who I am ...

Until you showed up in my life and showed me parts of me I didn't even know existed.

You were the light that illuminated the way to a better and brighter appreciation for who I am and showed me what I could be.

You made me want to evolve, each and every day – improving and evolving for the person who not only changed my life but my heart as well.

Thank you for so many things – but most of all, thank you for loving me when I didn't even know how to love myself.

You are and will always be ...

My one true thing and the best thing that ever happened to me.

My love, my soulmate, my twin flame.

Because of you, I'm able to believe in me, you and our future.

You showed me how to love in the most beautiful way of all –

Through your eyes.

I Can't Promise to Fix All of Your Problems, but I Can Promise You Won't Have to Face Them Alone

My Love ...
My promise to you on this day,
As on all the days to come ...
I can't make the rain go away,
Nor make the sun to shine again ...

But I can be your shelter through any storm.
I'll never have all the answers,
Nor always know the right way,
But I'll be there to share the walk
and hold your hand through the rain.

I can't promise easy days,
Nor times without struggle,
But I will be there for you,
Facing the world by your side.

I can't fix your problems,
Nor make them disappear,

But I can promise you ...
That come what may,

Until the stars fall from the heavens above,
The horizon melts away and time ceases to be,
That you'll never have to face the world alone.

May I always be the light that leads you home,
The smile that greets you at day's end,
My embrace holding you tightly,
Your safe place from all else.

I'll be your unending love, evermore,
Yours forever, faithfully.
As you fall asleep every night,
Know this to be true,
For now and always,
How very much I love you.

Thank You for Reminding Me What Butterflies Feel Like

There once was a time when butterflies
Were a dream I had never known.
I'd spent my days chasing the wrong ones,
Never letting the right one catch me.

When you start listening to your heart
And stop hearing everyone else,
You begin to give yourself a chance
To find real and lasting love.

They say that love shows up
When you least expect it,
And I never could have foreseen you
And how you changed my life forever.

The way you love me at my worst,
And celebrate me at my best.
Holding my hand through the storms,
Dancing with me in the rain.

I never knew I was lost until you found me,
Never realized I was incomplete
Until you made me whole.
Two hearts, one beat and a beautiful future.

Nights spent lost in your arms,
Days wrapped up in your heart,
Most of all, thank you for always reminding me
What butterflies feel like with your kiss.

You Make My Heart Smile When Nothing Else Can

When I told you this was forever,
I knew what we would face.
Falling in love is easy;
Staying in love isn't.
We make mistakes, we rise and fall,
So long as we face them all together …
The hard days, the truly challenging ones,
Won't tear us apart.
In fact, it's those storms of life that will bring us closer together.
When the rains come crashing down on your heart, know that I'm right there beside you,
Holding your hand and telling you everything will be okay.
We won't always have the answers and things won't ever be perfect,
But you'll always be perfect for me.
Protect, provide and profess:
I'll do all those for you and more.
Protect your heart as long as we both shall live.

Provide you with all the reasons to fall in love with me, all over again,
Every single day.
Profess my love for you through my words and actions …
Never will you doubt my loyalty and feelings for you.
So, let's make each other a promise:
To communicate through the problems,
To speak from the heart,
To smile through the pain,
To just be there for each other.
Home will always be your embrace.
In this life until there is no more,
That's all I could ever want and need.
Just you … forever.

To Truly Be in Love

Darling,

When I told you I had fallen in love with you, those words failed to encompass the depths of my feelings for you.

There may not be any words in any language that can encapsulate what you mean to me and how you've changed my life ... forever.

You whisked into my life from a world away, and I haven't been the same since – nor would I ever want to be.

Once you've been touched by the heart of an angel, how can you ever go back to the normalcy of a life without love?

One can't.

I won't.

Our love was unlike anything I'd ever known, though the meeting of our souls was so familiar – seemingly as if we'd loved in lives past and time beyond.

Sometimes ... you just know.

It's incredible because you don't know how you know ... only that you do.

A comfortable warmth that beckons you home – in those moments, you realize that you've found the mate of your soul in an unlikely way ...

But I'd have it no other way, would you?
The beckoning of an intimacy that defies reason, it's the catalyst for a passion that ignites every corner of your heart, mind and body ...

It permeates your thoughts and fuels your desires in a way that is strangely ... familiar.

No matter where we are or what the occasion, it takes only a subtle look from you, and in those moments, our eyes have an inviting conversation from across a room.

Swept away by your smile and intoxicated by the whisper from your heart, I cast aside judgement and reason as I reach your side.

Time slows and the world melts away as our lips collide and I pull you to me.

In that instant, as in all the time afterwards, you are all that matters.

You. Me. Us.

As I gaze into your eyes and wrap my arms around you, a conflicting peace envelopes my soul ...
While my senses are on fire ...
You, my love, are all I'll ever need.

Those Quiet Times When the World Just Melts Away

It's those quiet times,
At the end of our day,
When the rest of the world slowly fades away.
Those are the moments I'll always cherish.
My arms around you, soaking in the events of the day,
Sharing my life with you.
It's not that it's always excitement and thunder,
It's that I get to spend it with you.
Your smile.
Your embrace.
Your love.
Talking intimately with the woman I love,
Grasping you in my arms ...
It sets my soul on fire.
I wish I had a magic power in those fleeting instants,
That I could make time stop as I gaze lovingly
Into your eyes,
So that I could love you longer,
Hold you tighter,

And squeeze those beautiful times like a warm blanket that grants such peace.

As we turn the pages of our story, these are the memories that I'll never forget.

The moments that I fell in love with you all over again,

each and every time ...

... when I wished we could live forever

In those frozen moments of love.

I Want You Forever

They say there will be a moment when you know.

Across a crowded room, you glimpse at her, and all you see midst the crowds of people … is her.

Your only thought in that instant is that you have never seen anything so beautiful in your life.

Her smile and radiance drown out the world and all you know as your mind races is that you can't imagine spending your life anywhere else but in her arms.

There's no rationale or reason that overcomes you as your heart skips a beat and your breath stops – only the absolute truth that she is the one.

Despite the turmoil that surrounds you and the chaos of life that envelopes you at that split second:

that certainty – hers – calms your spirit and fills your heart.

In that moment, you realize that every bad choice and each failed relationship has led you exactly where you needed to be.

You'd gladly kiss all the frogs again and try to make all the glass slippers fit once more that were never meant to … because you had to experience all the wrong answers to understand the right one when it finally found you.

The ifs and questions slowly fade away,

All that you know with complete certainty is that you want to love her for the rest of your life.

So Much More than Those Three Little Words

They say that fairy tales aren't real and that dreams can't come true.

Things don't work out anymore for anyone and romance is dying … they'd have you know.

I never stopped chasing my dreams of love and wishing on stars that she'd show up ... and now I know why.

You can't make love show up before it's time and no amount of desire can alter what's meant to be.

It's hard, it's frustrating, but I know now that it's worth it – so very much so.

Looking into your eyes, I understand why all the others were all so wrong for me.

Hearing you say my name proved that all the naysayers never really "got it" about love, destiny and what's meant to be.

You can believe all your life that true love will find you, but until it does, it's just faith –

The hopes and dreams of fools, everyone would tell you.

Hoping that the one meant for you will show up is nothing more than a belief that you hold on to … deep down in your soul.

As time slowed and I felt your arms around me, I knew in that moment what "meant to be" truly felt like.

Come what may, from whatever broken road we may have traveled, all paths led us to each other.

That's not chance, hope or fortune.

All the heartache and broken promises just seemed to wash away as I pushed the hair away from your eyes.

In that moment, it all made sense.

You made everything … just make sense.

As if I'd known you, my love, all my life.

Almost as if I'd known the answer all along.

I turned to speak before you stopped me and smiled, saying simply …

"Of course."

In my heart, I knew you were perfect for me before I ever even asked.

Freeze Time

Darling,

No matter where we are,

There are those moments in which I wish I could just freeze time.

So I could steal away those beautiful emotions of being in your arms and tuck them away ...

Little pockets of sunshine and happiness,

The joy of loving you in those instants is immeasurable ...

I could live forever in the comforting embrace of your love,

Wrapped up in a feeling of bliss that would be endlessly enchanting.

There's nothing in this life so wonderful as the feeling of your love in my arms, against my skin and in my soul.

As our hearts beat in unison and souls collide,

My spirit soars with the knowledge that you'll always be at the beginning and ending of all my days, for there's nothing more precious and wonderful than your outstretched arms waiting for me.

Waking up next to you and falling asleep in your arms are two of the most amazing feelings I've ever known ...

And I get to experience them each and every day with the woman I love.

If I could capture that beauty of our love incarnate,

I would be a very rich man indeed ...

For having loved you would be the greatest treasure of all.

Yet no money nor possessions could ever compare to the blessing I found in you.

The most valuable thing I will have ever have ... is and will always be your love.

The Heart that Beats Only for You

I don't always have to tell you that I love you –
I show you in the ways that I love you and what
I do – for you, with you, because of you –
the ways I cherish you without fail.
I never meant to fall in love with you, but
from the first smile to your last giggle,
you pretty much ruined that plan ...
and I couldn't be more okay with it if I tried.
When I seek meaning, you give me reason.
When I lose my way, you lead me back home,
to your arms.
When I wonder what tomorrow holds,
Your kiss shows me the future and all that can
and will be.
In truth, that's all I've ever wanted:
Love in my heart, hope for my spirit and belief
in my soul.
When I found you?
I found all that and so much more.
Thank you for all that you are ...

Most of all, thanks for the love that you give,
the person that you are and how you protect
and celebrate my heart ...

That will always light the way to our brightest of
tomorrows.

You give rhyme to the reason,

Sanity to the madness.

I could try to count all the ways I love you, but
I'd rather just show you –

Each and every day,

For the rest of our lives.

That's just one of the many reasons why my
heart will always and forever beat ...

Just for you.

And I Wonder, How Did I Find One So Perfect for Me?

When the still of the night settles around us,
And you're lying quietly on my chest,
I just soak in the beauty of the moment:
Your almost angelic breaths rising and falling,
As you drift off in peaceful slumber,
That's just one more reminder of all the ways I'm thankful for you,
And simply can't believe that you're mine.
I watch you sleep and whisper all the things that sometimes escape me when we're together.
I wish I was better with my feelings and words sometimes, but I know you see how deeply I care for you in my eyes, in my actions and how I love you ...
How very much you mean to me,
How you've changed my life and bettered my world.
How much you make me feel loved and special and that every day
Is a joy and an adventure with you by my side.

Your soul found mine and together, we've never looked back.

I try to reminisce to a time before you,

And honestly, all of those thoughts and feelings escape me – almost as if they never even happened.

Truthfully, nothing could ever compare to what we found in each other and the love we share.

You're my true love, my everything and my safe place.

As I brush away the wisps of hair from your peaceful face,

I can't help but radiate a warm smile from my heart.

You found me in a sea of people and made me complete,

Against all odds in a way that could only be fate and destiny.

I didn't really know what love felt like before you showed me, and now I can't imagine a life where I don't wake up beside you every day.

You were the answer to the question I didn't know how to ask,

The hope that I didn't know to dream for,

And the miracle that I couldn't have imagined.

I didn't even know how lost I was until you came knocking on my door,

Pulling on my heartstrings in a way that no one else could.

As I kiss your forehead and let my lips linger,

I realize for the millionth time,

Just how very blessed I am.

I'll love you until the horizon meets the sky and the ending of time.

I smile as I slip away into sleep,

Knowing I'll awaken to the best thing that's ever happened to me … you.

Love Like Fairy Tales Do Come True

I don't care what "they" say.

I want a fairy tale.

I deserve happily ever after and once upon a time.

I need the love affair that will take my breath away.

They don't dare to dream.

I do.

I will have the love story that redefines the fairy tale.

Kisses in the rain and embraces in the dark.

Yes.

Chivalry is still alive and dreams do come true.

I want out of the labels into a class of my own – I don't believe in fitting into boxes, those are for the unimaginative.

"They" haven't kissed an angel – they don't know what forever looks and feels like.

I have.

Passionate kisses, warm hugs and the look in her eyes that melts my heart.

So, don't tell me I can't have an old fashioned romance that never ends ...

Because I can. I will.

I do.

The kind of love that people see and smile, because they know.

They don't have to ask how or if, they just get it – they can see it in our eyes.

She'll be the type of lady who lights up a room when she walks in and brightens my smile.

When I look at her from across the way, I know one thing: she's the one.

I won't settle for anything less, and I don't have to.

True love and forever are real if you just know how to believe and have faith ... and an open heart.

I believe in true love, in soulmates, in twin flames.

I believe that we find the one when we are meant to, chance doesn't tell us the ending to our story.

We do – if we are open-hearted and able to believe.

So, when I tell you I want the fairy tale, and the last first kiss ever, believe it.

I'm not asking anyone but one to share my dream, because "they" will never understand the true power of a love story like ours ...

And it's okay, no one else has to.

So long as I have you in my arms and our love in my heart, I know that we can do anything, together.

Until you catch a taste of heaven on the lips of an angel, you don't how amazing that kind of love truly is.

It doesn't just change the moment or the kiss, it transforms everything: your heart, your dreams and your life.

Once upon a time and happily ever after, our fairy tale love story started with a look and ended with forever.

You made all my dreams come true in a single kiss.

The next chapter ... in the rest of our lives.

Then, I'll find you sooner in the next life once more ...

So I can love you longer –

True love stories never end.

Forgetting Yesterday & Dreaming of Tomorrow

Once upon a time,
I didn't believe in fairy tales, true love or happily ever after.
I had been hurt more times than I could count,
Found all the dead ends in search of love.
It seemed that each time I got my hopes up,
They were dashed just as quickly.
I'd look around and see the couples in love, dismayed at the proclamations of feelings everyone else shared ...
That I seemed destined to never know for myself.
That's a lonely place, you know?
One piece of a jigsaw meant for two, even if you don't quite truly believe that you'll ever find "the one" ... it's hard to be solo when you're missing something you can't quite put your finger on.
So, you sing all the love songs, read all the love stories and wistfully make wishes on every shooting star.

You can be in a room full of people and feel utterly and completely alone.

Not that the others don't love you, make you feel unaccepted or leave you out ...

But it's just not the same as sharing it with that special someone.

You see, though, I never stopped believing that she was out there ...

And one afternoon, everything changed.

Left became right and up turned into down.

Truthfully?

I've never been so happy to be completely breathless as I was in those moments.

The moment I saw my future waiting for me as I walked through the door.

The moment I fell in love as I saw you for the very first time.

The moment I recognized what forever tasted like when I kissed your lips.

You see, it's in those life changing instants when you happen upon the one meant to share your life that all the failures of love lost and broken roads melt away.

The lonely nights and disappointment all just make sense as I take you into my arms and finally find refuge in the embrace that I've waited my entire life for:

Yours.

We'll look back many years from now and know that was the beginning of forever.

I told you that I would marry you on the very first night we met, and though you thought me crazy ...

Perhaps I thought so a little as well –

It turns out maybe I wasn't so crazy after all, because I recognized my future in you.

When you know ... you just know.

And as I fall asleep every night with your face resting on my chest, I couldn't be more thankful for the broken roads ...

That led me straight to you.

I Don't Want the Moon ... I Want to Love and Be Loved

Darling,

When I say that I love you,

I'm trying to say so much more than those three little words convey.

I'm trying to tell you how very special you are to me, how you mean more than anything else.

I'm trying to express how deeply I care for you, and how much I love the times we share.

I'm trying to share how much I trust you, need you and know that I'll always be there for you.

I'm trying to relate how much I depend on you and wouldn't want to face life without you.

There aren't words that can truly define the way I feel about you, but I hope you can tell –

In the way I look at you with complete adoration,

In the way I will always put your needs first,

And how very much I look forward to coming home to your arms.

In the way I think of you when you're not beside me,

with a love note, a text or a passing thought ...

You can't cross my mind because you never leave it.

So, each time that I take your face in my hands and smile,

Saying those three words that encompass so much more,

Know that "I love you" is my daily proclamation of how grateful I am for you, how much I appreciate all that you do for us,

And how I can't wait to spend the rest of my life loving you.

You are and always will be my forever person.

I love you.

Love Her So Much that She May Doubt Your Sanity ... But Never Your Passion

Before you came into my life,

I would never have believed there was a good kind of crazy – until you showed me differently.

You turned everything upside down and changed all the things I thought I knew about myself, life and love.

You made everything finally make sense in a way that I never knew was possible.

The wish I made for true love so long ago came true in you.

You drive me crazy – but in the best way,

and I wouldn't trade that for anything.

If my passion-infused devotion and lovingly-intense desire for you puts me on the edge just a bit ...

then I will gladly walk that line to spend a lifetime in your arms.

Call me crazy,

Call me passionate,

Call me intense,

Just so long as you always

Call me yours.

Hold My Hand and Don't Ever Let Me Go

I can't always promise days without storms,
Or nights without darkness.
But I can promise you won't have to face them alone,
My hand in yours,
Our hearts beating as one,
My home in your arms,
My love forever in your eyes.
In those moments of weakness,
When the world has gotten you down,
And life has taken its toll,
Take my hand in yours,
Meet my gaze with your eyes,
And hold fast to one truth:
I'll always be there, by your side, to weather any storm.
You're never alone, my love …
And you never will be again.
Hold my heart in yours,
Ours souls united …

And always know that we can overcome anything,
Together,
You and I as one ...
Forever.

True Love is Worth the Wait

I choose you and always will, from the first time I ever saw you to my last breaths that leave this life.

Every single day, through the happiness and the tears, I will always choose you –

to have and to hold,

to face all of life's challenges and victories,

to celebrate our life and our love ...

These are only a few of the many things that I choose, with you, for you and because of you.

They say that life is a series of choices made, and that may well be true,

but every closed door and failed love led me to your arms.

I'd say that I'd choose to go back and take away all the pain that the past caused you, but then the hurt and the angst only made you into the beautifully broken and wonderfully strong person that I love today.

I choose to share our moments, both big and small, to make the memories that will leave our hearts full and our souls content.

It seemed like an eternity waiting for you – and I always knew you were right around a corner someday, so I fought to always believe and never lose hope in you, in me, in us.

I choose you to build a life with, chase dreams beside and love forevermore, for that is our blessing that I will always cherish, never doubt and ever be thankful for.

As much as I'd like to say that I chose you all along, our love story was written in the stars long before our souls ever reunited.

Meant to be, happily ever after, all the phrases that couples utter doesn't begin to tell our tale of two souls that found a way to each other despite the distance, the odds and the broken roads that threatened to tear us apart.

So, as I take your face in my hands and drink in your soulful eyes, know that you gave me hope when I had little, purpose when I searched for mine, and a love that has shown me the happiness that I never knew was possible.

I choose you, every day, in every way, to fall in love with all over again.

I choose to give you my heart, mind and soul as I always have, until the end of days.

It's a choice that is and always will be the foundation of the life we built together, the dreams we share and the love affair that never ends.

Our love story.

No matter how long I may have waited to find you, I'd wait countless lifetimes again to have the chance to love you once more.

I love you.

To Laugh Forever with Someone You Take Seriously

Have I told you lately that you're just my kind of weird?

Before you, I always felt like I was the only one with my kind of sense of humor – a little different, sometimes twisted, always lively.

I've never been able to have an entire conversation with someone else through a single look ...

Until you.

All my jokes that no one else ever gets, you do in a way that just makes me smile.

The funny and unique glances across the room between us speak volumes.

We speak our own language – words and phrases that no one else in the world would ever understand ...

And that's the beautiful thing about us:

They don't have to.

You just get me in ways I can't explain, and I wouldn't trade that for anything.

You can finish my sentences and understand a single look.

In fact, we can hold an entire conversation with just a solitary glance.

That's something that's very rare and wonderful.

Maybe it's strange that sometimes you know what I want even before I do.

But that's not something I want to ever change.

My true love showed up with mismatched socks, a crooked halo and warped sense of humor.

I wouldn't want it any other way.

That's the real magic of having your very own unique fairy tale.

It starts in your own style and ends with your own special happy ending.

I didn't see you coming, and I never could have imagined a love like ours ...

But I'll always smile when I remember how much I'm loved by you.

I Need You with Me

I was never a person to miss someone.

I valued my independence and celebrated my solitary life ...

Until you showed up and decided to turn my world upside down.

Love doesn't even begin to describe the depth of us, and missing you falls short of saying how much I need you with me.

There aren't adequate words in any language that I can find that will ever convey how I feel about you.

The moment when my lips part from yours and I leave your side, wistful ...

Is the split second I feel incomplete.

You don't cross my mind ...

You never leave it.

Yet, we're never truly apart,

for I carry you with me, tucked away safely in my heart.

No matter how hard my days may be or how life can wear me down,

I know that I have something special waiting for me.
Your arms, your smile, your love.
For even at my weakest, you hear the song in my heart and sing it back to me when I forget the words.
I could write a thousand love stories and countless fairy tales, and yet nothing my pen could weave ...
Would ever compare to what you mean to me.
My best friend, my soulmate, my forever love.
You're my happy place ...
Thank you for being you.
It's changed my life, my heart, my future.
Right now ...
I just need your arms around me.
That's one of the feelings I love the most.
I love being in love with you.

The One Who Completes You

And then, all of the love songs were about you
...
Now, I almost can't remember life before you and how I was ever happy any other way but in your arms.

Some things are just meant to be – you made me understand that from the moment we met
...
Now I can't and won't see my life and my future any other way.

I fell in love with you, and now I know why this is the greatest feeling I've ever experienced.

There's no place that I'd rather be than in your heart.

Her Anchor, His Wings

He's something she's never known –
A safe place for her heart, a harbor midst any storm that she might face.
He's her rock, her strength, her reason.

She's unlike anyone he's ever met,
She sparkles when she talks,
She shines when she smiles,
Her light infuses brightly into his very soul.

He does more than dance with her demons,
He soothes her deepest fears with his touch.
Her moods and battles just seem to balance out
When he places his hand in hers.

He didn't know what it meant to not be alone,
Used to standing strong and living solo,
He wasn't used to someone who would be there,
Supporting him like she does through it all.

He lives in a way that makes her pulse race,
Invigorating her spirit with his fearless attitude,
He brings her to edge of the wild before
Whispering to her soul of love's promise.

She brings a peace to his heart he's never found,
A place of rest that whispers to him in the quiet,
Telling him it's okay to be himself, to be loved,
That he's safe with her, in her arms, forever.

No matter her flights of fancy,
Regardless where her mind may wander,
When she's settled back to earth,
She knows the solace she found in him, her anchor.

He never knew how to chase his dreams,
Let his hopes and spirit soar with the heavens
Until she showed up and made him realize,
Sometimes you have to find the wings you had all along.

They were a pair unlike any other,
Checks and balances, yin and yang.
They completed each other like a jigsaw puzzle,
Found each other against impossible odds,
Believing when love seemed so far away,
They discovered the most unlikely thing in an improbable way.

The perfectly imperfect love of two people
Who never gave up on the dream that
One day, they too,
Would find their happily ever after.
They found that and so much more ...
In each other, now and for always.

Every Time She Laughs

Why am I so madly in love with you?

It's so much more than your beauty or what you say, more than your adorable smirk or the clever quips you make.

I'm at a loss for words to describe the effect you have on me ...

It's in the way you smile,

the twinkle in your eye and even in the way you carry yourself.

Your charm, your personality, your heart and soul ...

There are so many reasons why I'm so enamored with you that I'd like to spend the rest of my days enjoying you.

Truth is, I've decided simply to embrace every day and show you in countless ways the amazing blessing you are to me ...

To appreciate the person you are and everything you mean to me.

When you smiled, you had my attention.

When you talked, you captured my mind.

When you laughed, you stole my heart.

When you looked in my eyes, you won my love forever.

I thought making you laugh would undoubtedly make you fall for me,

but every time I hear that mischievous and beautiful giggle, I can't help but fall in love with you all over again.

Me and you,

Laughing, loving and living our best life ...

The essence of every dream I've ever had for what real love would truly be.

That's my promise and hope for every tomorrow.

Until then, I'll simply drink in the beautiful hue of your sparking eyes,

I'll smile at your joyful laughter,

And most of all,

I'll embrace you with every part of my heart, mind and soul.

Just know this:

You'll always find me waiting for you ... on the steps to forever,

Loving you, endlessly.

Love Itself Isn't Enough to Make Forever Possible

Most of us think happily ever after is just a story of butterflies and happy times, and it is ...

But it's so much more than that.

It's a tale of devotion, respect, love and communication.

I knew when I realized that I fell in love with you,

That was just the beginning.

The happiness and warm fuzzy feelings of love are amazing,

But there's so much more.

Anyone can fall in love, but it takes work to stay in love.

It requires loyalty and commitment,

passion and effort and never being lazy or selfish in love.

Putting each other first, doing what's best for ourselves and each other, and never forgetting the love in our hearts.

Our relationship started with love,

was built with trust and respect,

And was strengthened by work and communication.

Sometimes, it's more than the big moments that take our breaths away, but all the little ones as well.

Sometimes, saying "I'm sorry" isn't to admit fault,

But rather to express that the relationship is more important than your ego.

I'll never lose my love and desire for you,

Our passion will always be kindled in your eyes.

I know that forever takes work … every day.

I can't just tell you that I love you.

I have to show you.

Love and compassion through action and selfless virtue.

Romance and passion have their place,

But it's what we do when we face the world together that matters.

Hand in hand, we can overcome anything so long as we communicate,

Learn to compromise,

And understand each other's needs.

We will never be perfect,

Nor will our relationship.
But with hard work and lots of love,
We will always be perfect for each other.
So, let's make a promise to each other, here and now –
Let's always fall in love, all over again ...
Every ... single ... day.

Now and For Always

Promise me this, for now and always:

Promise me your heart, to have and hold, 'til life takes my last breath.

Promise me your love, until the whisper of time slips away.

Promise me your passion, so we may always know the fire that unites our hearts.

Promise me your soul, so that I may uncover all that you are 'til the end of our days.

Promise me kisses to welcome me home,

Hugs to remind me I'm safe and

Your touch to assure me it'll all be okay.

Promise me to share all the big moments as well as all the little ones in between.

Promise me to always stand beside me, facing every storm and challenge, hand in hand.

Promise me your respect, and I'll do the same.

Promise me your first thought daily and your last as you drift off to sleep …

And may a smile find you as you think of me.

Those are but a few of the promises I'll cherish from you,

As well as the promises I will make:

I promise to love you without question,

be loyal without end and be yours without fail.

I promise to love you, now and always, for who you are and who you will always be.

I promise to always be your best friend, your soulmate and forever love ...

unconditionally, until we find each other in the next life.

I promise now and for always ...

To love you, endlessly.

We Will Always Be My Favorite Love Story

Life isn't always going to have great events and exciting times.

It's those quiet moments we spend together, just the two of us, stolen away from the world that we will truly cherish.

Everyone always says you'll remember the big things – the anniversaries and events, the grand to dos of a life well lived.

But as I look over at you, your hand nestled softy on my arm, I realize those aren't the only feelings that I'll carry in my heart.

It's times like this, the frozen moments that make my soul content as my heart sighs.

Limbs entangled and your beautiful smile illuminating the night, these are the moments that matter most to me … the ones that I'll forever cherish.

With you by my side and love in my heart, there is nothing more priceless than being wrapped up in your arms.

So, let's celebrate the fireworks and flash,

but always remember it's the time we spend together in the still of the night, quiet and full of love ...

these are the deepest and most heartfelt keepsakes of our life together.

Waking up to see you walk into the room dressed in my oversized dress shirt makes my heart smile in ways I had never dreamt possible.

Thank you for being you ... and more than anything,

Thank you for sharing this life and this love with me.

You will always be my baby, my princess, my lady and greatest triumph.

You showed me a way and a depth that I had never seen or felt before ...

And now, nothing else makes sense without you.

You're my rhyme, my reason, and my one true thing.

You showed me a life and a love that I never thought possible.

More than anything, when I'm with you, everything just makes sense.

I love you ...

More today than yesterday and never as much as I will tomorrow ...

Always and forever.

We Will Always Be My Favorite Love Story

Ravenwolf

Find more love, hope and empowerment at
www.houseofravenwolf.com
including Ravenwolf's complete works
and quote merchandise.

Sometimes life gives you a fairy tale. You just have to believe.

www.ingramcontent.com/pod-product-compliance
Lightning Source LLC
LaVergne TN
LVHW041940070526
838199LV00051BA/2853